A Day at the **Beach**
Animal Life on the Shore

Rock Stars

Limpets, Barnacles, and Whelks

by Ellen Lawrence

Consultant:

Professor Steve Hawkins
University of Southampton
Southampton, England

Marine Biological Association
Plymouth, England

BEARPORT
PUBLISHING

New York, New York

Credits

Cover, © Ria K/Shutterstock, © 2009fotofriends/Shutterstock, and © Chris Moody/Shutterstock; 2, © Picture Partners/Shutterstock; 4T, © Paul Heinrich/Alamy; 4B, © Natural Visions/Alamy; 5, © Shelly Beach/Shutterstock; 6, © carolyn/Shutterstock; 7, © B. Borrell Casals/FLPA; 8, © Simon Colmer/Nature Picture Library; 9, © Steve Trewhella/FLPA; 9R, © Steve Trewhella/FLPA; 10, © taveart/Shutterstock; 11, © Paul S. Wolf/Shutterstock; 11B, © Steve Bloom Images/Alamy; 12, © D P Wilson/FLPA; 13, © Barrie Watts/Getty Images; 14, © D P Wilson/FLPA; 15, © Choksawatdikorn/Shutterstock; 16, © Nigel Sawyer/Alamy; 17, © Frank Hecker/Alamy; 18, © Nick Upton/Nature Picture Library; 19, © Juniors Bildarchiv GmbH/Alamy; 20, © Ian Smith; 21, © Gerald Marella/Shutterstock; 21R, © Joshua Davis Photography; 22L, © Steve Taylor ARPS/Alamy; 22R, © Michael Krabs/Imagebroker/FLPA; 23TL, © alexilena/Shutterstock; 23TC, © D P Wilson/FLPA; 23TR, © Dan Bagur/Shutterstock; 23BL, © Cheryl Ann Quigley/Shutterstock; 23BC, © Steve Trewhella/FLPA; 23BR, © Stevenson/Shutterstock.

Publisher: Kenn Goin
Senior Editor: Joyce Tavolacci
Creative Director: Spencer Brinker
Photo Researcher: Ruth Owen Books

Library of Congress Cataloging-in-Publication Data in process at time of publication (2018)
Library of Congress Control Number: 2017048989
ISBN-13: 978-1-68402-446-9 (library binding)

For more information, write to Bearport Publishing Company, Inc., 45 West 21st Street, Suite 3B, New York, New York 10010. Printed in the United States of America.

10 9 8 7 6 5 4 3 2 1

Contents

The Tide Comes In

At a warm, sandy beach, there are **tide pools** surrounded by rocks.

Covering the rocks are thousands of shells.

They are home to limpets, barnacles, and whelks—the tide pool's rock stars.

When the tide comes in, these animals disappear beneath the water.

Then it's time for the rock stars to come to life!

limpets and barnacles clinging to a rock

a barnacle feeding

At the seashore, the ocean comes in and goes out twice a day. The rising and falling of the water is known as the tide.

tide pool

5

A Rocky Life

Limpets are sea snails that live on the tide pool rocks.

A hard, cone-shaped shell protects a limpet's soft body.

The sea animal chooses one rock to be its home for its entire life.

It uses a large, muscular foot to hold on tight to the rock.

limpets

A limpet's shell grows in a way that lets it fit tightly to the rock. If the rock is softer than the shell, the limpet grinds away the rock with the edges of its shell to make a better fit.

the underside of a limpet

mouth

large foot

Can you think of why a limpet might cling to a rock?
(The answer is on page 24.)

Sea Supper

Once the tide comes in, it's safe for a limpet to let go of its rock.

Underwater, it crawls around looking for food.

It feeds on seaweed and other kinds of **algae**.

When the tide starts to go back out, the little creature returns to its home spot.

It hugs its rock tightly until the tide comes back in.

a limpet feeding

algae

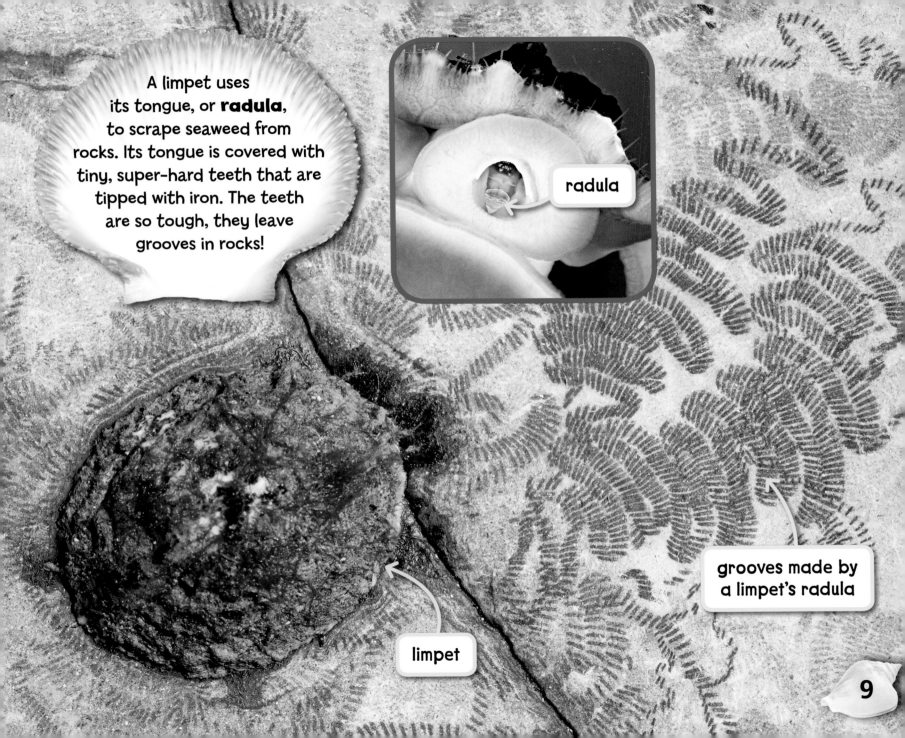

A limpet uses its tongue, or **radula**, to scrape seaweed from rocks. Its tongue is covered with tiny, super-hard teeth that are tipped with iron. The teeth are so tough, they leave grooves in rocks!

radula

grooves made by a limpet's radula

limpet

9

Meet Some Barnacles

Limpets live alongside tiny neighbors called barnacles.

These little rock stars stay in one spot and never move.

A barnacle has a soft body and a hard shell.

At the top of its shell is a tiny trapdoor.

Once a barnacle is underwater, it opens its trapdoor.

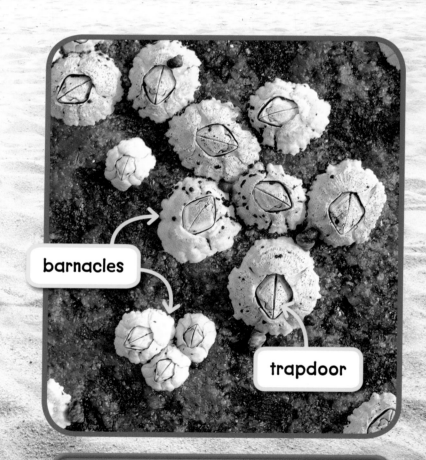

barnacles

trapdoor

What do you think happens once a barnacle opens its trapdoor?

Barnacles don't only live on rocks. Sometimes, thousands of barnacles will make their home on a whale or the bottom of a boat!

humpback whale

barnacles

Grabbing a Meal

A barnacle opens its trapdoor so it can catch food.

From inside its shell several feathery legs appear.

The barnacle's legs act like a net, catching tiny bits of food floating in the water.

When the tide goes out, the barnacle closes its trapdoor again.

This keeps the creature from drying out.

A barnacle mostly eats tiny animals and plants called plankton. These living things are so small, they can only be seen with a microscope.

plankton

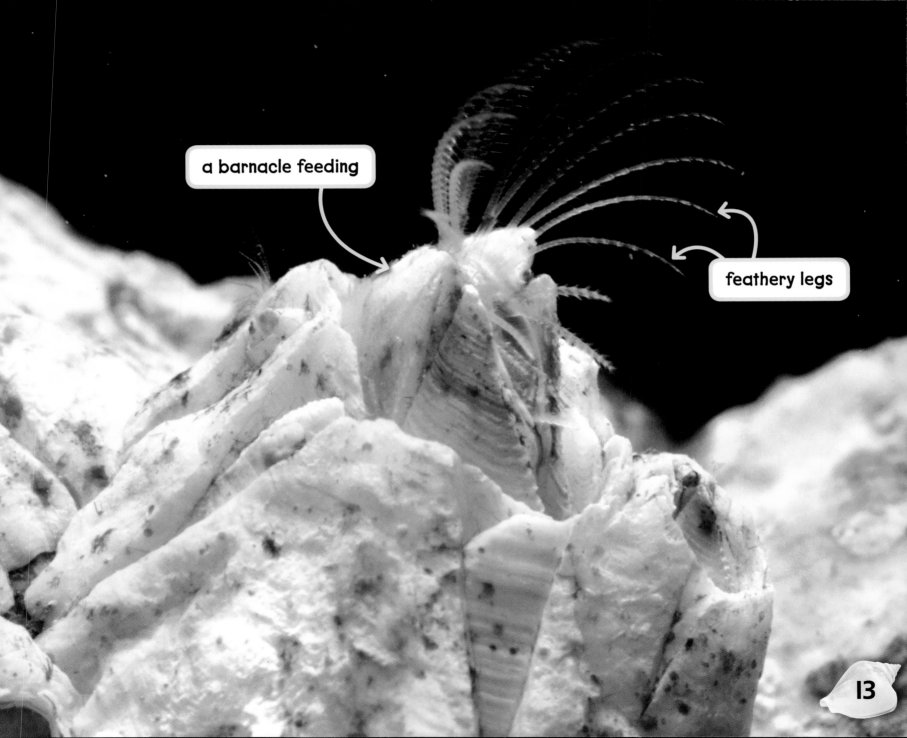

a barnacle feeding

feathery legs

13

Baby Barnacles

When it's time to have young, barnacles **mate** with neighboring barnacles.

After mating, one of the barnacles produces eggs.

Once the eggs hatch into **larvae**, the little creatures float away.

Over time, they grow and change shape.

Finally, they are ready to cling to a rock and grow an adult shell.

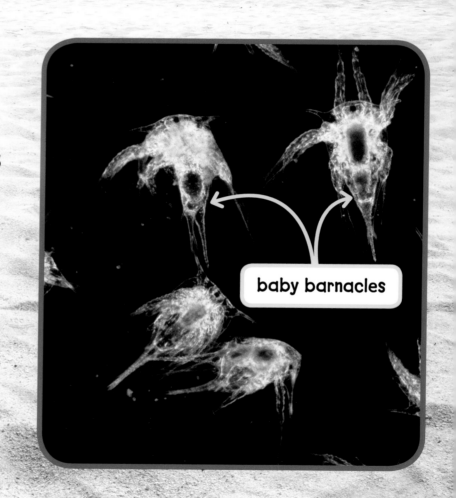

baby barnacles

A Whelk Attacks!

A hungry **predator** called a dog whelk is feasting on barnacles.

Using its radula, it drills a hole right through a barnacle's hard shell.

Next, the whelk dribbles a chemical into the shell that turns the barnacle's soft body to mush.

Finally, the whelk sucks up its soupy meal!

empty barnacle shells

dog whelk

a dog whelk
hunting for food

siphon

A dog whelk
is a kind of large sea
snail. It slides over rocks
in the ocean, sniffing for
food with a long body
part called a siphon.

17

Hundreds of Eggs

In or around tide pools, male and female whelks meet up to mate.

Then the female whelk lays bunches of egg capsules.

She attaches the capsules to a rock.

Each capsule contains up to 100 tiny eggs!

There are many different types of whelks. Some are the size of a grape. The largest is the trumpet whelk, which can grow more than 2 feet (61 cm) long.

whelk egg capsules

female whelk

egg capsules

19

Baby Rock Stars

Inside their egg capsule, tiny baby whelks hatch.

The first babies to come out of their eggs feed on their brothers and sisters.

Then the little whelks break out of their capsule.

They are ready to hunt and live on their own as ocean rock stars!

This baby whelk is smaller than a grain of rice. It's born with a shell, which grows over time.

Seabirds, crabs, fish, and even people eat whelks. If a predator attacks, a whelk tucks its whole body inside its shell.

a seagull eating a whelk

a whelk hiding inside its shell

Science Lab

Be a Shellfish Scientist!

We know a lot about limpets, barnacles, and whelks because scientists have studied them for many years. Now it's your turn to investigate! Read the following questions and write your answers in a notebook.

1. Look at the picture below. What do you think made the circle on the rock and why?

2. Look at the tiny gray lumps on the shells of the dog whelk and limpet in the picture. What do you think the lumps could be?

3. Choose one of the animals in this book, and then answer the following questions:

- *What does the animal eat?*

- *How does it find, gather, or catch its food?*

(The answers are on page 24.)

Science Words

algae (AL-gee) plantlike living things, such as seaweed, that mostly grow and live in water

larvae (LAR-vee) the young of some animals, including shellfish and insects

mate (MAYT) to come together to have young

predator (PRED-uh-tur) an animal that hunts other animals for food

radula (RAJ-oo-luh) a hard, rough tongue covered with tiny teeth

tide pools (TIDE POOLZ) small pools on a beach where water remains once the tide goes out

Index

Read More

Oldfield, Dawn Bluemel. *Patterns at the Seashore (Seeing Patterns All Around)*. New York: Bearport (2015).

Owen Ruth. *Welcome to the Seashore (Nature's Neighborhoods: All About Ecosystems)*. New York: Ruby Tuesday (2016).

Spilsbury, Louise. *Tide Pool (Look Inside)*. North Mankato, MN: Heinemann (2013).

Learn More Online

To learn more about rock stars, visit **www.bearportpublishing.com/ADayAtTheBeach**

About the Author

Ellen Lawrence lives in the United Kingdom. Her favorite books to write are those about nature and animals. In fact, the first book Ellen bought for herself when she was six years old was the story of a gorilla named Patty Cake that was born in New York's Central Park Zoo.

Answers

Page 7: A limpet holds on tight to its rock to keep itself from being knocked from its home by waves. A limpet also clings to its rock to avoid being eaten by predators.

Page 22:

1. The circle on the rock is a limpet's home. The animal made the circle after grinding away the rock with its shell. It did this to get a tight fit between the rock and its shell.

2. The lumps on the whelk and limpet's shells are baby barnacles.